D0492116

00 400 830 913

LIFE IN AN
EGYPTIAN TOWN

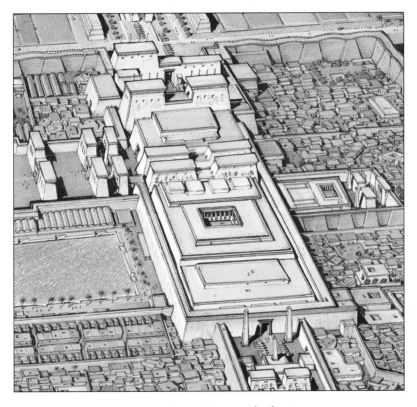

JANE SHUTER

Heinemann
LIBRARY

First published in Great Britain by Heinemann Library,
Halley Court, Jordan Hill, Oxford
OX2 8EJ, part of Harcourt Education.
Heinemann is a registered trademark of Harcourt
Education Ltd.

Produced for Heinemann Library by
    Bender Richardson White
Editor: Lionel Bender, Nancy Dickmann, Tanvi Rai
Designer and Media Conversion: Ben White and
    Ron Kamen
Illustrations: John James, Jonathon Adams and
    Jeff Edwards
Maps: Stefan Chabluk
Picture Researcher: Cathy Stastny and
    Maria Joannou
Production Controller: Kim Richardson and
    Séverine Ribierre

Originated by Ambassador Litho Ltd
Printed in China

ISBN 0 431 113025 (hardback)
09 08 07 06 05
10 9 8 7 6 5 4 3 2 1

ISBN 0 431 113106 (paperback)
10 09 08 07 06
10 9 8 7 6 5 4 3 2 1

British Library Cataloguing in Publication Data
Shuter. Jane
    Life in an Egyptian town. - (Picture the past)
    932
A full catalogue record for this book is available
from the British Library.

Acknowledgements:
The publishers would like to thank the following for
permission to reproduce photographs: Ancient Art
and Architecture/John P. Stevens p. **25**; Ancient Art
and Architecture/R. Sheridan pp. **8**, **12**, **15**;
Committee of Egypt Exploration, London p. **24**;
Corbis Images Inc. p. **30**; Heinemann Library pp. **16**,
28; Peter Evans p. **27**; Robert Harding Picture Library
p. **6**; Trustees of the British Museum p. **18**, **21**, **22**
(numbers EA10057/8-PS177397, EA-15671-PS213448,
EA26780-PS343512); Werner Forman Archive/Dr. E.
Strouhal p. **14**, **17**; Werner Forman Archive/Museo
Egizio, Turin p. **23**;Werner Forman Archive/The British
Museum, London p. **13** (number PH1033A); Werner
Forman Archive/The Egyptian Museum, Cairo pp. **7**,
10, **19**, **20**, **26**.

Cover photograph of a wooden model of a
carpentry workshop with craftsmen at work
reproduced with permission of Werner Forman
Archive.

Every effort has been made to contact copyright
holders of any material reproduced in this book. Any
omissions will be rectified in subsequent printings if
notice is given to the publishers.

Any words appearing in bold, **like this**, are
explained in the Glossary.

www.heinemann.co.uk/library
Visit our website to find out more information
about **Heinemann Library** books.

To order:
📞 Phone 44 (0) 1865 888066
📠 Send a fax to 44 (0) 1865 314091
💻 Visit the Heinemann Bookshop at
    www.heinemann.co.uk/library to browse our
    catalogue and order online.

ABOUT THIS BOOK

This book is about daily life in towns in ancient Egyptian times, which lasted from about 3100 BC to 30 BC. The ancient Egyptians lived in towns and villages along the River Nile. Most of Egypt is desert. The climate is hot, with very little rain. Ancient Egyptians could live in Egypt only because the Nile gave water for farming, drinking and washing, and it flooded each year. When the flooding went down, it left behind rich soil for growing crops. Towns and villages were always close to the Nile, which was used for transport, too. Many townspeople were farmers.

We have illustrated this book with photographs of objects from ancient Egyptian times and artists' ideas of town life. These drawings are based on information about ancient Egyptian towns that has been found by **archaeologists**.

The author

Jane Shuter is a professional writer and editor of non-fiction books for children. She graduated from Lancaster University in 1976 with a BA honours degree and then earned a teaching qualification. She taught from 1976 to 1983, changing to editing and writing when her son was born. She lives in Oxford with her husband and son.

Contents

Egyptian towns

Ancient Egyptian towns were large settlements. They grew up in places where there were important **temples**. They also grew up around palaces for the **pharaoh**, the ruler of Egypt, or where the **officials** who helped him to run the country lived. Towns were busy, noisy places. Tall houses were crowded together, making the narrow streets shady to walk along. The streets were dirty and smelly, too. They were full of rubbish that people threw away, because there was no rubbish collection.

Look for these:
The pharaoh and his wife show you the subject of each double-page chapter in the book. The model of a house shows you boxes with interesting facts, figures and quotes about ancient Egyptian towns.

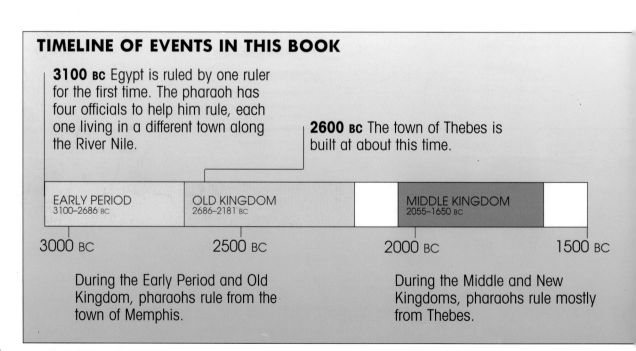

TIMELINE OF EVENTS IN THIS BOOK

3100 BC Egypt is ruled by one ruler for the first time. The pharaoh has four officials to help him rule, each one living in a different town along the River Nile.

2600 BC The town of Thebes is built at about this time.

| EARLY PERIOD 3100–2686 BC | OLD KINGDOM 2686–2181 BC | | MIDDLE KINGDOM 2055–1650 BC | |

3000 BC — 2500 BC — 2000 BC — 1500 BC

During the Early Period and Old Kingdom, pharaohs rule from the town of Memphis.

During the Middle and New Kingdoms, pharaohs rule mostly from Thebes.

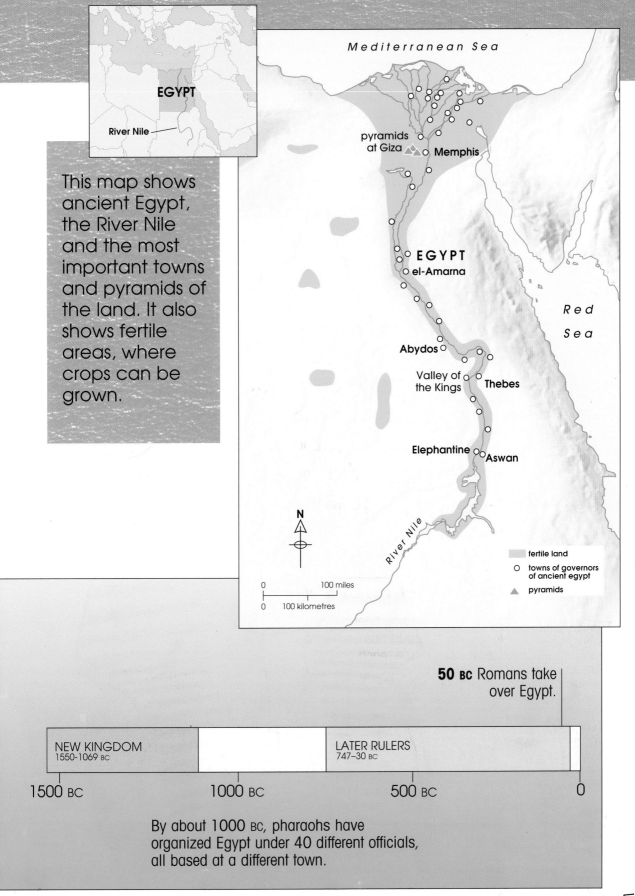

EGYPT

River Nile

This map shows ancient Egypt, the River Nile and the most important towns and pyramids of the land. It also shows fertile areas, where crops can be grown.

Mediterranean Sea

pyramids at Giza

Memphis

EGYPT

el-Amarna

Red Sea

Abydos

Valley of the Kings

Thebes

Elephantine

Aswan

N

River Nile

0   100 miles

0   100 kilometres

fertile land

○ towns of governors of ancient egypt

▲ pyramids

50 BC Romans take over Egypt.

NEW KINGDOM 1550-1069 BC		LATER RULERS 747–30 BC	

1500 BC   1000 BC   500 BC   0

By about 1000 BC, pharaohs have organized Egypt under 40 different officials, all based at a different town.

The pharaoh's palaces

The **pharaoh** lived in a palace in the town he wanted to rule from – his capital or main site. Thebes and Memphis were most often used as capitals.

Other big towns had palaces for the pharaoh to use as he travelled. Some **temples** also had palaces, built on one side of the temple buildings. This was because the pharaoh ran the religion of Egypt, too. Palaces always had a wall around them, to keep them separate from the rest of the town.

Pharaohs owned beautiful things and these were buried with them when they died. This mask of gold and gemstones was put on the pharaoh Tutankhamun when he was buried in 1327 BC.

The palace had many different rooms, gardens and pools. Some parts of the palace were used only for important occasions, such as visits from foreign rulers. All the palace was beautifully decorated, inside and outside. The mud bricks were plastered over and painted white. Then they were painted with colourful scenes of birds in the marshes, or scenes that showed how powerful the pharaoh was.

MUD BRICKS

All ancient Egyptian houses were built from mud bricks, even the pharaoh's palaces. The only stone buildings were the temples, although stone was also used for the outside of some of the **pyramids** – the tombs of some of the pharaohs.

Ancient Egyptians, even pharaohs, did not have much furniture. But the furniture they did have was beautiful. This bed and chair belonged to the mother of the pharaoh Khufu.

Temples

Most towns had at least one **temple**. Temples were the only stone buildings and were beautifully carved and painted. They were built as homes for the gods and goddesses of ancient Egypt. Some temples were huge, with their own workshops, workers' houses and farmland. Others were no bigger than a house. Sometimes several gods and goddesses shared a temple. Ordinary people could not go into temples. **Priests** and **priestesses** were allowed in, to serve the gods and goddesses.

LAVISH TEMPLES

An ancient Egyptian carving on a temple describes how it was decorated: 'The temple was built from white stone. The floors were lined with silver. Its doorways were decorated with a mixture of gold and silver.'

In this painting, a sem-priest, on the left, is at a funeral. Sem-priests carried out all the ceremonies at burials. They always wore a leopard skin – no other priest did.

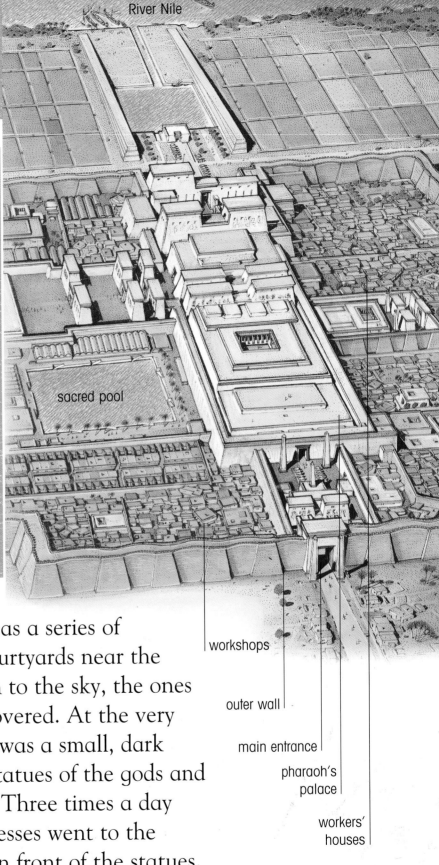

River Nile

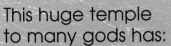

This huge temple to many gods has:
- a wall around it
- courtyards in a line from the main entrance to the River Nile (in the background)
- a palace for the pharaoh, with its own outer wall
- a sacred pool, for the priests to wash in before worshipping the gods
- workshops and workers' houses.

sacred pool

workshops

outer wall

main entrance

pharaoh's palace

workers' houses

Temples were built as a series of **courtyards**. The courtyards near the entrance were open to the sky, the ones at the back were covered. At the very back of the temple was a small, dark **shrine** room with statues of the gods and goddesses inside it. Three times a day the priests or priestesses went to the temple to worship in front of the statues.

Shopping

Towns did not have shops. The ancient Egyptians lived simply and did not have many possessions. But they needed cooking pots, clothes and baskets. People did not use money, but swapped spare food or things they had made for items they needed.

This swapping is called bartering, and it was how all trade was carried out in ancient Egypt. People had an idea of what things were worth related to the price of a lump of metal, usually copper or silver. Important people had more food, land, animals and possessions to swap.

Traders brought in expensive things from other countries, such as wood, jewels, spices and animal skins. They brought them to the town by boats along the Nile. Only the pharaoh or important people could afford expensive goods.

SWAP!

When Hay, a worker at the town of Deir el-Medina, bought an ox from the local policeman, he swapped it for:

- two jars of fresh fat
- five tunics of smooth cloth
- a skirt of thin cloth
- an animal skin.

Sometimes people bartered with neighbours and friends. If a friend did not have a spare **tunic**, ox or basket to swap, they might know someone who did. But people also bartered at markets that were held regularly, usually at the docks by the river, where there was a big open space. People laid out what they had to barter on mats on the ground.

Markets like this one were held in the open air. People often put up cloth **awnings** to give them some shade from the Sun.

Homes

Ancient Egyptian homes were built to cope with the hot, dry weather. They were built from mud bricks. Town houses were built two or three storeys high, and squashed together in rows.

Houses had small, high windows with wooden shutters and openings in the roof to let in some air. Inside, rooms were often dark, cramped and airless, and had very little furniture. Everyone used their roof as a living space. People spent more time on the roof, often under an **awning**, than indoors.

Important people had gardens with ponds, like the one shown on this ancient Egyptian wall painting . Like gardens, ponds were expected to be useful as well as beautiful. People ate the ducks and fish kept in them, as well as admiring them.

SHADY GARDENS

Because Egypt was so hot and dry, gardens and plants were a luxury. Water for them had to be brought from the river. The gardens had trees that gave shade and food, for example date palms and pomegranate trees.

Because there was less space in towns, people who wanted a lot of room had to build upward, so there were many tall, thin houses. This is a model of a house with three storeys, found in a tomb.

Ordinary people painted their homes white inside. More important people had more rooms, more furniture and more space. They had elaborate wall paintings, especially in the room they used for entertaining. They had toilets and washrooms, but no drains. They collected the washing water and toilet waste to put on the fields. Ordinary people just used the fields as toilets and washed in the river.

Using the river

The ancient Egyptians built most of their towns close to the River Nile because they needed its water every day. The flooding of the Nile gave them the rich, muddy soil to grow their crops, which needed daily watering from the river, too. The ancient Egyptians used water from the Nile to make the bread and beer that everyone ate and drank. Workers needed water to make mud bricks and clay pots. People washed, bathed and swam in the river.

DIRTY LAUNDRY

Most people had their washing done for them, as homes did not have running water. Washing was done in the river, by men, not women. A **scribe** wrote: 'The washerman washes on the shore, while the crocodile lurks near by.' It was seen as a dangerous job.

Bakers made dough from grain flour and water from the Nile. They kneaded the dough then placed it in clay moulds. These were baked in ovens heated by burning wood.

The River Nile provided food as well as water. The ancient Egyptians ate fish and wild birds more often than they ate domestic animals, such as sheep and cattle. The Nile was also the most important way of travelling around Egypt, as towns were built along the river. This included short journeys, since there were few roads or tracks through the desert.

Boats were important to people going up and down the River Nile. People also needed them to cross the river, as there were no bridges. Boatmen ran regular ferry trips.

Work

Every big town had craft workshops for potters, furniture makers, metalworkers, glassmakers, weavers, leather workers and jewellers. Men did these jobs. Women from important families looked after their homes and children. Women from ordinary families worked as servants, or in spinning and weaving workshops. They also worked baking bread and brewing beer.

The most skilful workers worked in the big workshops that belonged to the pharaoh or to important officials, or were attached to temples.

Most townspeople, whatever their jobs, worked for the **temple** or the important town **officials**, or even the **pharaoh**. As well as their ordinary work, everyone who was not a **scribe** had to do **duty work** for the pharaoh. This was often building work, hauling stone for temples or tombs, or constructing new houses in the town.

Making bricks was an important job in ancient Egypt. Houses and palaces were built from mud bricks, which crumbled over time in the heat. They regularly needed repairing. Brickmakers mixed mud and straw together, then pressed the mixture down into a wooden frame. Most bricks were dried out in the hot Sun.

All towns needed brickmakers. Their mud bricks were similar in size to the grey concrete blocks that house builders use today on the insides of walls.

Education

This is part of the ancient Egyptian *Rhind Mathematical Papyrus,* which was used to teach scribes. It shows how to work out the angles of **pyramids**.

In ancient Egypt, most children did not go to school. Reading and writing were skills that only the children of **scribes** were taught. These boys and girls were taught from the age of five, at a school in the **temple** or in a town **official's** home. They were learning to run the country for the **pharaoh**, so they had to learn maths, too.

Some sums from scribe school:

- Fat worth 10 gallons of grain has been given to you. You have to make it last a year. How much can you use each day?
- A granary bin is 5 cubits long, 5 cubits deep and 5 cubits wide. Will 10 gallons of grain fit into it?

[A cubit is an ancient measure – the length from an adult's elbow to the tip of the middle finger.]

This ancient Egyptian model shows a weaving workshop where all the workers were women. Weaving was one of the few trades that women were allowed to do.

Usually, boys were taught their father's job. From the age of about five, the sons of craftsmen began to help their fathers at work in the home. They fetched and carried, then did simple tasks. A few years later, most of them would become **apprentices** in the workshops where their fathers worked.

Mothers taught girls how to run a home. If their mothers worked in a bakery or a weaving workshop, girls sometimes learned this skill, too.

Play

Even though children started to work from the age of five onwards, they still played together in their spare time. Ordinary children in towns spent a lot of time playing together outside, not in their cramped homes. They played with balls made from pieces of leather stitched together and stuffed with dried grass. Some of these balls have survived from 2500 years ago. Most pictures from the time show boys playing separately from girls.

Some tomb models show children at work, like the two boys (top right) in this furniture-makers' workshop. The boys would have begun work by sweeping up the workshop and fetching and carrying for the older workers.

The **pharaoh's** children did not play on the streets with ordinary children. They played in the palace. Children from important families played at home, too. Their homes had more space and gardens to play in. The girls had beautiful dolls made from wood, with arms and legs that moved. Girls from ordinary families had stiff wooden dolls, or dolls made from clay.

Many outdoor games in ancient Egypt were similar to those played today. Children raced each other and played chasing games. An ancient Egyptian carving showing boys playing tug-of-war has one boy shouting to the other, 'My side is stronger than yours!'

This toy once belonged to the child of an important family. The string makes the cat's mouth open and close.

Clothes

Egypt is very hot, so all Egyptians dressed to keep cool. Children wore nothing but sandals until about the age of ten. Everyone else wore clothes made from **linen**. Townspeople and villagers wore the same kinds of clothes. Ordinary working men just wore a short piece of cloth wrapped around their hips like a short skirt, or tucked between their legs like baggy underpants. Ordinary women wore a **tunic** to at least their knees.

JEWELLERY

Men, women and children wore jewellery. Poor people wore copper rings or a string of beads. The more important a person was, the more jewellery they wore. They wore jewelled belts, earrings, rings, bracelets and 'collars' – deep, flat necklaces that fastened at the back.

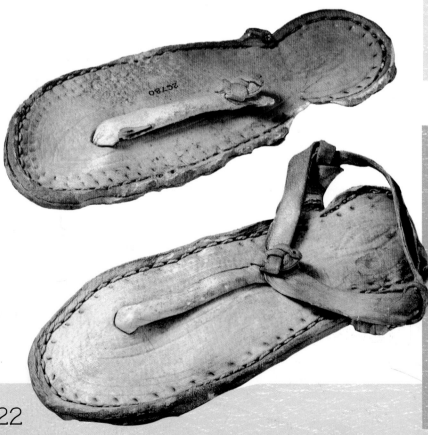

Only the leather sandals worn by important people have survived for us to study. Ordinary people wore sandals made from old reeds or other plant stems – or they went barefoot.

People kept their make-up in pots stored in wooden boxes, or in baskets.
This beautifully painted box belonged to an important lady.

Important people wore thinner linen cloth, bleached very white to reflect the sun. The thin cloth took longer to make. Women wore long tunics, and men wore tunics that came to the knees or to the ground. Often these clothes had lots of folds and pleats. They were harder to move freely in, and were more likely to get caught on things. They were for people who did not have to do hard work.

Important people wore lots of make-up and jewellery. Ordinary townspeople and villagers could not afford make-up and had only cheap jewellery.

Health and hygiene

The ancient Egyptians believed in keeping clean. They washed daily with water from the river, and washed their clothes regularly. They often shaved their heads, sometimes their whole bodies, with razors made from **bronze**. Many homes had a bathroom where people stood on a stone slab and poured water over themselves. They had no soap, but scrubbed themselves with a salt called natron. The water drained into a big bowl and was emptied on the fields.

Only important people had a stone toilet seat like this one. Most were made of wood. The seat was laid over a pottery jar that was emptied at least once a day. Poor people had no toilets and had to use the fields.

SAFE IN THE WATER?

The ancient Egyptians used a mixture of practical and magical ideas to keep healthy. So they taught their children to swim, which was practical, living so close to the River Nile. They also made their children wear magic charms to save them from drowning. It was important to do both these things.

Most towns had several doctors and a surgeon working with them. We know how these doctors worked because some of their medical books have survived. Doctors used herbal cures on their patients. For example, they gave willow bark pills for pain. Willow has the same chemicals in it as modern aspirin. At the same time as they gave the herbal cures, doctors said a magic spell over the patient.

This detail of a carving shows an ancient Egyptian surgeon's tools. Surgeons dealt only with serious disorders or injuries, as people knew surgery was dangerous and likely to kill the patient.

Religion

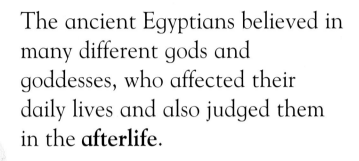

The ancient Egyptians believed in many different gods and goddesses, who affected their daily lives and also judged them in the **afterlife**.

The important gods and goddesses had several jobs. For example, the goddess Hathor was the goddess of love and also of music and childbirth. It was important to keep these gods and goddesses happy. This is why people built **temples** from stone – because the gods would need them to live in for ever.

Gods and goddesses were important to the ancient Egyptians. So was preparing for the afterlife. People were buried with *shabti* figures like this one, to do their work in the afterlife.

This boat was buried next to the pyramid of the pharaoh Khufu, as part of the treasure for him to take to the afterlife.

Everyone believed that as long as they had led a good life in this world, they would be rewarded after death. They were buried with possessions for the afterlife. The **pharaoh** had the most beautiful and expensive possessions. The **pyramids** of Egypt are tombs for some pharaohs. Each tomb is mostly underground, with many false passages and blocked walls, to stop people robbing the treasure inside. Ordinary people were simply buried in the hot desert sand.

Food

Ancient Egyptian townspeople all ate a lot of bread and drank a thick, weak beer made from stale barley. They had more choice of what to eat than people in small villages, because they could swap food. They ate onions, cucumbers, beans and other vegetables each day. They kept sheep, goats and cows for milk and cheese. Only the **pharaoh** and important people ate meat each day.

When animals were killed, they had to be eaten quickly, before the heat made the meat go bad. This ancient Egyptian wall painting shows animals being butchered.

Egyptian recipe – nut sweets

This recipe for sweets probably comes from the very end of the ancient Egyptian period. It was written on a piece of broken pottery. As few women – who mostly did the cooking – could read or write, most recipes were just memorized, not written down.

WARNING: Ask an adult to help you with the cooking.

You will need:
130 g of chopped dates
some hot water
a pinch of cinnamon
30 g of walnuts (or pecan nuts), chopped
1 tablespoon of honey
2 tablespoons of ground almonds

1 Mush up the chopped dates with about a teaspoon of hot water. Mix the mush until it is quite smooth.

2 Stir in the chopped nuts until they are well mixed with the dates.

3 Take a teaspoon of the mixture at a time and shape it into a ball. If it is too sticky, add some ground almonds.

4 Put the honey on a plate and roll the balls in it until they are coated in honey all over.

5 Now roll the sticky balls in the ground almonds.

Egyptian towns now

Egyptian towns are still mainly strung out along the River Nile. Many of them are built on top of, and around, ancient towns. The mud brick buildings have crumbled and been replaced many times over thousands of years. Modern towns are full of concrete and stone buildings. A **dam** has been built on the Nile, to stop the yearly flooding. So towns have been able to grow and move right down to the riverbanks.

The **pyramids** near the modern capital of Egypt, Cairo, were built almost 4500 years ago. They housed tombs for the **pharaohs** who ruled from the nearby ancient town of Memphis.

Glossary

afterlife imaginary world, where life was pleasant, to which ancient Egyptians believed they went following death

apprentice young person who works with an experienced craftsperson to learn a skill such as shoemaking

archaeologist person who uncovers old buildings and burial sites to find out about the past

awning cloth cover to keep off the Sun or rain

bronze tough, strong metal made by melting together two softer metals, copper and tin

courtyard open space within, or on one side of, a building

dam wall built across a river to hold back the flowing water. Dams often have gates or pipes to let through some of the held back water a little at a time.

duty work set number of days each year that people had to work for the pharaoh. Scribes did not have to do it.

linen fabric made from stems of the flax plant

official person who helps run a country

pharaoh ruler of ancient Egypt

priest/priestess man/woman who works in a temple, serving a god or goddess

pyramid tomb for a pharaoh, built between about 2650 BC and 1750 BC. Before and after this, pharaohs were buried in different kinds of tombs.

scribe person who could read or write

shrine room in a temple (or house) with statues of gods and goddesses to which people come to pray and leave gifts

temple place where people pray to gods and goddesses

trader person who buys and sells things that other people have made

tunic T-shirt-shaped clothing that came to at least just above the knee, worn by men, women and children

More books to read

Ancient Egypt: Builders and Craftsmen, Jane Shuter (Heinemann Library, 1999)

Ancient Egyptian Children, Richard Thames (Heinemann Library, 2002)

Ancient Egyptian Homes, Brenda Williams (Heinemann Library, 2002)

The Life and World of Tutankhamun, Brian Williams (Heinemann Library, 2002)

Visiting the Past: Valley of the Kings, Rob Alcraft (Heinemann Library, 1999)

Index

Titles in the *Picture the Past* series include:

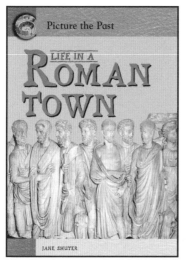

| Hardback | 0 431 11299 1 |

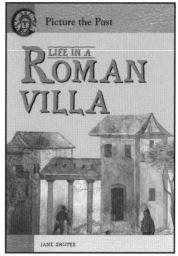

| Hardback | 0 431 11300 9 |

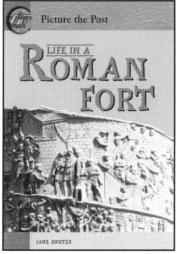

| Hardback | 0 431 11298 3 |

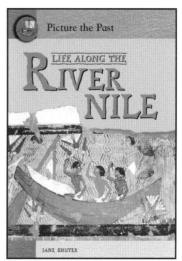

| Hardback | 0 431 11303 3 |

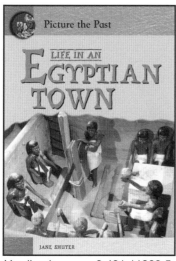

| Hardback | 0 431 11302 5 |

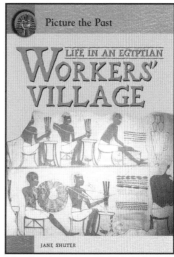

| Hardback | 0 431 11304 1 |

Find out about the other titles in this series on our website www.heinemann.co.uk/library